BRIDE OF
THE FAR SIDE

BRIDE OF THE FAR SIDE

Gary Larson

WARNER BOOKS

A *Warner* Book

First published in Great Britain in 1987 by Futura Publications
Reprinted 1989, 1990, 1991
This edition published by Warner Books in 1992
Reprinted 1993 (twice), 1994, 1995

A CIP catalogue record for this book
is available from the British Library.

ISBN 0 7515 0592 7

Printed and bound in Great Britain by
BPC Hazell Books Ltd
A member of
The British Printing Company Ltd

Warner Books
A Division of
Little, Brown and Company (UK)
Brettenham House
Lancaster Place
London WC2E 7EN

BRIDE OF
THE FAR SIDE

"Well, there is some irony in all this, you know . . . I mean
we BOTH lose a lens at the same time?!!"

Elephant skyways

"And now . . . Can dogs really talk? . . . We found one who's willing to try, right after this message."

"Hey! . . . Six eyes!"

"Listen . . . I'm fed up with this 'weeding out the sick and
the old' business . . . I want something in its prime."

"Now calm down, Barbara ... We haven't looked everywhere yet, and an elephant can't hide forever."

"Say, there's something wrong here ... We may have to move shortly."

"Well, okay, Frank . . . Maybe it IS just the wind."

"Wait a minute! Just wait a minute! No need to worry . . .
According to this, we're dealing with a rhino MIMIC!"

"Dang! . . . Sorry, buddy."

"Thunderstick? . . . You actually said, 'Thunderstick?' . . .
That, my friend, is a Winchester 30.06."

"Dibs."

Confused by the loud drums, Roy is flushed into the net.

"For the one-hundredth time in as many days! . . . I HAVEN'T GOT A QUARTER!"

Paramecium humor

"You fool! 'Bring the honey,' I said . . . This isn't the same thing!"

"Well, you've overslept and missed your vine again."

"I've got an idea . . . How many here have ever seen
Alfred Hitchcock's *The Birds*?"

"What the . . . ANOTHER little casket!!?"

"Well, I dunno, Warren . . . I think your feet may be uglier than mine."

March 5, 1984: After several months, I now feel that these strange little rodents have finally accepted me as one of their own.

Snake dreams

"Aaaaaaa! . . . It's George! He's taking it with him!"

"And now Edgar's gone . . . Something's going on around here."

Unwittingly, Palmer stepped out of the jungle and into headhunter folklore forever.

"Now you've done it!"

"Good heavens, Charles! You're at it again! . . . And with
my fresh sponge cake, I see!"

"Well, here we all are at the Grand Canyon . . . But, as usual, Johnny just had to ruin the picture for everyone else."

The boy who cried "no brakes"

Early vegetarians returning from the kill

"Ladies! Ladies! He's back! . . . Our mystery man who does the Donald Duck impression!"

"Cannonbaaaaaaaalllllllll!!"

"Okay! I'll talk! I'll talk! . . . Take two sticks of approximately equal size and weight — rub them together at opposing angles using short, brisk strokes . . ."

"Quit complaining and eat it! . . . Number one, chicken soup is good for the flu — and number two, it's nobody we know."

"Don't listen to him, George. He didn't catch it . . . The stupid thing swerved to miss him and ran into a tree."

The Squid kids at home

Rats! We're getting nowhere fast!.. The long end has to go up higher!

Listen!.. What if I come around to the other side or something?..

He's still there!.. Ow! Hey! You idiots!

"I tell you she's drivin' me nuts! . . . I come home at night and it's 'quack quack quack' . . . I get up in the morning and it's 'quack quack quack.'"

Hank knew this place well. He need only wait . . . The deer would come, the deer would come.

"Uh-uh-uh-uh-uh . . . Question. Can anyone here tell me what Hanson there is doing wrong with his elbows?"

"Uh-oh."

"Relax, Worthington . . . As the warm, moist air from the jungle enters the cave, the cool, denser air inside forces it to rise —resulting in turbulence that sounds not unlike heavy breathing."

"No lions anywhere? . . . Let me have the chair."

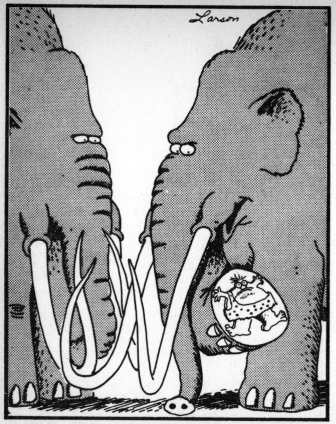

"Well, what the?... I THOUGHT I smelled something."

"Well, you've got quite an infestation here, ma'am ... I can't promise anything, but I imagine I can knock out some of the bigger nests."

Another sighting of the Loch Ness dog

"Now calm down there, ma'am . . . Your cat's gonna be fine . . . just fine."

"For crying out loud, Norm. Look at you . . . I hope I don't
look half as goony when I run."

"Ool . . . Here he comes to feed on the milk of the living."

Lost in the suburbs, Tonga and Zootho wander for days —
plagued by dogs, kids, and protective mothers.

"Dennis, do you mind if Mrs. Carlisle comes in and sees
your rhino tube-farm?"

The first cruise arrow is tested.

The mysterious, innate intuition of some animals

"Fire!"

"Okay, Wellington. I'm comfortable with my grip if you are
. . . Have you made a wish?"

"Oh, give me a home, where the buffalo roam . . ."

Testing whether laughter IS the best medicine

Jungle apparel

"No, Zak . . . It Wilga's turn lick bowl."

"I hate this place."

At night, the forest custodians would arrive — sometimes stopping to laugh and gossip about the habits of certain daytime animals.

When imprinting studies go awry

"Oh, no, he's quite harmless . . . Just don't show any fear
. . . Squids can sense fear."

"Play him, Sidney! Play him! . . . Ooooooweeeee! . . . It's gonna be fresh burgers tonight!"

Natural selection at work

"Well, she's done it to me again . . . Tuna fish!"

"That's the third one you've lost this month, Edgar . . .
You've got to stop believing these guys who say they're
just stepping out to use the restroom."

Dinosaur cranial capacity

Animal lures

"You know, it's really dumb to keep this right next to the cereal . . . In fact, I don't know why we even keep this stuff around in the first place."

Animal samaritans

"Hey, you stupid bovines! You'll never get that contraption off the ground! . . . Think it'll run on hay? . . . Say, maybe you'll make it to the moooooooon! . . ."

"Yes! Yes! This is it, Sidney! The guy with the dog! . . . I think he sees us!"

"Spiders, scorpions, and insecticides, oh my! . . . Spiders, scorpions, and insecticides, oh my! . . ."

And then, the dawn is still again — and another miracle of nature emerges.

Early musical chairs

tsetse fly

bullhead

booby

platypus

sapsucker

Clarence

Unfair animal names

Returning from vacation, Roy and Barbara find their house, their neighborhood, their friends — in fact, all of Atlantis — just plain gone.

Harvesting the work of ketchup bees

Suddenly, his worst fears realized, the old
fellow's tusks jammed.

People who don't know which end is up.

Early Pleistocene mermaids

"No gophers, Stuart . . . But there's an old garden rake of yours down here."

"Oo! Grog run into a . . . a . . . Dang! Now which kind stick
up and which kind hang down?"

"Let's move it, folks . . . Nothing to see here . . . It's all over
. . . Move it along, folks . . . Let's go, let's go . . ."

Her tentacles swaying seductively in the breeze, the
Venus Kidtrap was again poised and ready.

What dogs dream about

"Yes . . . I believe there's a question there in the back."

Harold would have been on his guard, but he thought the old gypsy woman was speaking figuratively.

Sixty-five million years ago, when cows ruled the earth

"I'm leaving you, Charles . . . and I'm taking the grubs with me."

Andrew is hesitant, remembering his fiasco with the car of straw.

"My word! I'd hate to be caught outside on a day like this!"

"Just pull it off and apologize, Cromwell . . . or we'll go out in the hall and establish this pecking order once and for all!"

"Polly wanna finger."

"Now listen! You both know the rules, you've got equal portions, and we're going to settle this thing once and for all . . . On your mark . . . Get set . . ."

"I just CAN'T go in there, Bart! . . . Some fellow in there and I are wearing the same hat!"

"Just a minute, young man! . . . What are you taking from the jungle?"

"It's Henderson again, sir . . . He always faints at the sight of yolk."

"Trapped like rodential"

"Hey! C'mon! Hold it! Hold it! . . . Or someone's going to get hurt."

"And, if you squint your eyes just right, you can see the zork in the earth."

"First!"

"Well, there it goes again . . . Every night when we bed down, that confounded harmonica starts in."

Stupid birds

"Oo! Watch out! . . . The walls are pointy!"

"Wait a minute! Isn't anyone here a real sheep?"

"Sorry, mister . . . but this is what we do to cattle rustlers in these parts."

"You idiot! . . . Now this time wait for me to finish the first 'row, row, row your boat' BEFORE you come in!"

"Yes, yes, already, Warren! . . . There IS film in the camera!"

"Now this next slide, gentlemen, demonstrates the awesome power of our twenty megaton . . . For crying out loud! Not again!"

"Hey! Look at Red Bear! . . . Waiiiiiiiit . . . THAT not real!"

"I've heard all kinds of sounds from these things, but 'yabba dabba doo' was a new one to me."

"I see your little, petrified skull . . . labeled and resting on a shelf somewhere."

"Oo! Goldfish, everyone! Goldfish!"

Charles wanders into a herd of dirt buffaloes.

"My turn . . . Well, I'm originally from the shores of the upper Nile and . . . saaaaaaay . . . Did anyone ever tell you your pupils are ROUND?"

"Look out, Larry! . . . That retriever has finally found you!"

Common medieval nightmare

"C'mon, c'mon, buddy! The heart! Hand over the heart!
. . . And you with the brains! . . . Let's have 'em!"

"Well, Bobby, it's not like you haven't been warned . . . No roughhousing under the hornet's nest!"

"My word! . . . That one came just too close for comfort, if you ask me."

"Mrs. Harriet Schwartz? This is Zathu Nananga of the Masai . . . Are you missing a little boy?"

"Your room is right in here, Maestro."

"No more! No more! I can't take it! . . . That incessant buzzing sound!"

"There! There! See it, Larry? . . . It moved a little closer!"

"Feeding frenzy!"

"Oh c'mon now . . . I know! Why don't you two go downstairs today and build a monster?"

"Gee whiz . . . You mean I get a THIRD wish, too?"

"Say, Carl . . . Forget the Hendersons for a second and come look at this thing."

"Late again! . . . This better be good!"

Stimulus-response behavior in dogs

"I knew it! I just knew it . . . 'Shave-and-a-Haircut' was a lousy secret knock."

"Yes, with the amazing new 'knife,' you only have to wear
the SKIN of those dead animals."

History and the snake

"Well, Zoron . . . is THIS a close enough look for you?"

Primitive peer pressure

"Say . . . wasn't there supposed to be a couple of holes punched in this thing?"

"And see this ring right here, Jimmy? . . . That's another time when the old fellow miraculously survived some big forest fire."

"Nothing yet . . . How about you, Newton?"

"Hey! . . . You kids!"

"Reuben! The Johnsons are here! You come up this
instant . . . or I'll get the hose!"

"Grunt, snort . . . grunt grunt, snort . . ."

Where parakeets come from

"Mom! Edgar's making that clicking sound again!"

"Egad! . . . It's got Uncle Jake!"

"I assume you're being facetious, Andrews . . . I distinctly yelled 'second' before you did."

"So, Billy! Seems your father and I can never leave without you getting yourself into some kind of trouble!"

"Mind if we check the ears?"

"Well, you better get someone over here right away . . .
He really looks like he's going to jump."

"Well, there it goes again . . . And we just sit here without
opposable thumbs."

"Hey! You'll get a kick out of this, Bob and Ruth! . . . Watch what Lola here does with her new squeeze doll!"

"These little ones are mice . . . These over here are hamsters . . . Ooh! This must be a gerbil!"

"Okay, before you go, let me read this one more time: 'Burn the houses, eliminate the townsfolk, destroy the crops, plunder their gold!' . . . You knuckleheads think you can handle all that?"

"For crying out loud! . . . We were supposed to turn south after that last mountain range!"

"Trim the bowl, you idiots! Trim the bowl!"

"Don't shush me — and I don't care if she IS writing in her little notebook; just tell me where you were last night!"

Dreaming he's falling, Jerry forgets the well-known
"always-wake-up-before-you-land" rule.

"Guess who!"

"Me? I WAS charging on the right, when you suddenly went left, so I went left, and then you went right again, you idiot!"

One day, as he nonchalantly reaches for a match, Leonardo da Vinci's life is suddenly transformed.

In the animal self-help section

"Well, I beg your pardon . . . But where I come from, it's considered a compliment to let fly with a good trumpeting after dinner."

"For heaven's sake, Elroy! . . . NOW look where the earth is! . . . Move over and let me drive!"

"What have I told you about eating in bed?"

"Take me to your stove? . . . You idiot! Give me that book!"

Other titles by Gary Larson.
To order these or other Warner titles, please see the following page

BEYOND THE FAR SIDE	£4.99
THE CHICKENS ARE RESTLESS	£5.99
COWS OF OUR PLANET	£5.99
THE FAR SIDE	£4.99
THE FAR SIDE GALLERY	£7.99
THE FAR SIDE GALLERY 2	£7.99
THE FAR SIDE GALLERY 3	£7.99
THE FAR SIDE GALLERY 4	£7.99
THE FAR SIDE GALLERY 5	£8.99
THE FAR SIDE OBSERVER	£4.99
HOUND OF THE FAR SIDE	£4.99
IN SEARCH OF THE FAR SIDE	£4.99
IT CAME FROM THE FAR SIDE	£4.99
NIGHT OF THE CRASH TEST DUMMIES	£4.99
THE PREHISTORY OF THE FAR SIDE	£9.99
UNNATURAL SELECTIONS	£5.99
VALLEY OF THE FAR SIDE	£4.99
WIENER DOG ART	£5.99
WILDLIFE PRESERVES	£4.99
THE CURSE OF MADAME "C"	£5.99

All Gary Larson's titles published by Warner Books can be ordered from the following address:

Little, Brown and Company (UK),
P.O. Box 11,
Falmouth,
Cornwall TR10 9EN.

Alternatively you may fax your order to the above address.
Fax No. 01326 317444

Payments can be made as follows: cheque, postal order (payable to Little, Brown and Company) or by credit cards, Visa/Access. Do not send cash or currency. UK customers and B.F.P.O. please allow £1.00 for postage and packing for the first book, plus 50p for the second book, plus 30p for each additional book up to a maximum charge of £3.00 (7 books plus).

Overseas customers including Ireland, please allow £2.00 for the first book, plus £1.00 for the second book, plus 50p for each additional book.

NAME (Block Letter) . . . .

ADDRESS . . . .

. . . .

☐ I enclose my remittance for _____

☐ I wish to pay by Access/Visa Card

Number [ ][ ][ ][ ][ ][ ][ ][ ][ ][ ][ ][ ][ ][ ][ ]

Card Expiry Date [ ][ ][ ][ ]